II

Trump is the Least Bad

No Aces for the 2016 Presidential Election

Alejandro Hector Ochoa Gonzalez

𝕿rump is the Least Bad

No Aces for the 2016 Presidential Election

1.
THE RACE FOR THE PRESIDENCY

It has been said that politics is the second oldest profession.[1] I have learned that it bears a striking resemblance to the first.

—Ronald Reagan (1911-2004)

The 2016 Presidential Race has been politically anemic, and has weak and bad candidates —namely, liar and master manipulator Hillary Clinton (Chicago, 09/26/1947-), and unpredictable and zigzagging entrepreneur Donald Trump (Queens, New York City, 06/14/1946-).

---

1. Journalism is the third oldest profession, and as well as the oldest and the second oldest professions, it is a necessary evil.

How far they are from Calvin Coolidge, the 30th President of the U.S. (1923-1929)!

Hitherto the electoral race has been theatrically intense, plentiful in disqualifying adjectives thrown by non-candid candidates at each other, like "crooked", "corrupt", "unfit".

The least bad nominee is entrepreneur turned politician Donald Trump, and now he is sailing speedily, thanks in part to the Britain's exit (Brexit) —decided on Thursday, June 23, 2016—, no matter that tricky surveys and bent polls show "advantages" for Clinton.

These two individuals are following on their respective paths to success, the ultimate goal of some American politicians: becoming President of the United States.

Until now, there have been 44 Presidents of the United States, seemingly a small number, but commonly logic and adequate for a rare, sometimes prestigious and always elusive charge.

One example of a politician who never reached his maximum goal is that of Hubert H. Humphrey, Jr. (1911-1978), 38th Vice President of the U.S. (from January 20, 1965 to January 20, 1969).

For many others, id est, common people, chasers of the American dream, success can mean starting their own business and thrive, acquiring a big house with a garden, buying a state-of-the-art smartphone, living happily with their family, doing tours to Europe, et cetera. But for a politician, the supreme act of realization would be serving his/her country from the apex of the bureaucratic pyramid.

Whichever the result may be after some 130 million citizens vote, and 538 electors cast their ballots on Tuesday, November 8, 2016, it will add to the costs of economic uncertainty and volatility.

The silent majority and the American people in general will have to pay for it.

The current hopefuls do their best to appear confident and cheerful, with well rehearsed optimism in speeches and rallies, undoubtedly they have shown they possess leadership and convening power, but the task will be translating all of those assets toward the transformation of American society.

How each of them become able to communicate the people that they are correctly interpreting the **desires** (maybe not the actual **needs**) of citizens will take one of them to the tip-top of the pyramid.

Democratic candidate Hillary Clinton chooses which questions asked by journalists, interviewers, she will answer and which not. For example, she has not answered some questions about her emailgate —official, secret and top-secret emails stored on a private server in the basement of her home in Chappaqua, New York when she was Secretary of State—[2], Wall Street...

She is an attorney at Law (ack!); most of her life, she has been a "**budgetivore**". Hers are low-quality credentials.

Negative points for her. ⌐

For one thing, Trump is trying to avoid all kinds of deviationism, after having won easily the Republican nomination. ⌐

Also, his political incorrectness is good for the country and for him. The U.S. has

---

2. The Federal Bureau of Investigation (FBI) director, James Comey, on Tuesday, July 5, 2016, recommended no criminal charges against Hillary Clinton for her "extremely careless" handling of classified information while she was secretary of State.

Comey also declared that a person still employed by the government —Hillary Clinton left the State Department in 2013— could have faced disciplinary action for doing what she did.

Aside, specialists could assume that she will not be prosecuted, not only because currently she is not a public employee, but for the reason that there was not intent or bad faith to harm national security on her part, two seemingly necessary conditions in order she could be prosecuted.

had enough of euphemisms. It is time to call things by their name again.

In caucuses and primaries, Donald Trump won by getting many votes from big conglomerates such as white males, and white females as well, who have no doubt about their belonging and acceptance. They need a strong leader, a good ruler.

A chameleonic politician, it seems that, at last, he's moving in the right direction in the Right party.

Sometimes, his lack of synderesis is evident, though there is no premeditation in his acts.

He has outlined an electoral program and a political and economic platform that will have to move the needle on the needs and problems of the nation.

The probable electoral success of Donald Trump would be based on some of the following foundations:

(A) The increasing level of Trumpmania.

(B) His honesty and political incorrectness, both of them alluring.

(C) He is by far more telegenic and likeable than Clinton.

(D) Even some distorted, emotional or naïve perception by Americans as for the real financial and economic outcome the Brexit may render could be beneficial for Trump's electoral odds, and results.

■

Given that since 1975 the nonsense, anti-Western bias, ravings and rampant mismanagement of the infamous and calamitous United Nations Educational, Scientific and Cultural Organization (UNESCO) have increased, as well as those of governments and brazen imitators, unthinking followers, civil society organizations (CSOs) or non-governmental organizations (NGOs), pseudo-progressive individuals, snobs and cronies, gutter press, mercantilist radio stations and television networks which sometimes follow leftist agendas, it would make sense that the next Federal Administration, criticize and exert more pressure over the UNESCO, a devalued organization, plagued by costly and almost useless bureaucrats who act and maneuver in order to benefit themselves and pro-socialist governments.

The U.S. actually withdrew from the organization in December, 1984. It rejoined in 2003, and in 2013 deprived the UNESCO of about 22 percent of its funding; as a consequence, the United Nations' cultural arm, headquartered in Paris, suspended American voting rights.

■■■

According to the October 1977 issue of the Chicago-based *Specialty Salesman Magazine* (now defunct), the twelve most persuasive words in the marketing and selling world were/are:

1. save
2. money
3. you
4. new
5. health
6. results
7. easy
8. safety
9. love
10. discover
11. proven
12. guarantee

How many times have you lately heard one, two or more of these words uttered by Trump, or Clinton during their political marketing efforts?

Well, maybe they have not literally expressed some of these words, but please let us pinpoint something: they have made some equivalent paraphrasing:

1. When they have spoken about taxing less low-class families, perhaps they are meaning something like, hey, fellow Americans, I will make you **save**.

2. "American economy", "large tax cut", "tax relief", "Increasing the tax burden on wealthy individuals and big corporations…" are phrases deeply related to **money**.

3. Politicians make their best efforts to serve **you** —U.S. citizens.

4. Each candidate tries to show the people a (supposedly) **new** path.
5. **Health** issues are a main concern for U.S. citizens.

6. **Results**. The past of each one of them can speak respectively about him and her.

7. **Easy**. There are no easy roads for politicians, especially in a real democracy, but people can have an **easy** living ahead, as sweet as a cherry tablet which is dissolved in the mouth, and then nothing's left.

8. **Safety**. Radical Muslims are attacking here and there, and want to destroy the United States of America.

9. I **love** you people of the U.S., please hark onto me, because I will be your savior.

10. Look at me, **discover** that I am a suitable politician, and I am the right individual for the Oval Office.

11. I have shown you what I can do; I have **proven** that with my deeds; I will take care of you.

12. I **guarantee** you a flawless tenure.

XVIII

2.
POLITICS

Firstly, let's consider how and why the U.S. has lately come to the current difficult condition.

A main factor has been constituted by some mismatched perspectives between the Executive and the Legislative branches of the Nation.

One of the biggest problems is how to fine tune the bad and noisy channels of intercommunication among legislators and presidents and Cabinet members.

Have you ever imagined a Government where the messages and the communication between those two branches of Power were smooth and seamless?

For, something which should be strange, but nevertheless is common, happens daily around the world:

Some people wish to communicate something, but between them and the listeners huge information asymmetries can take place.

The former are aware of certain issue or matter or regulations, or even dominate them at their fingertips, but the latter do not know what those other do.

Executives/managers – employees,
teachers – students,
politicians – voters,
rulers – citizens,
salesmen/vendors – customers (or
        prospective customers)
doctors – patients,
writers/journalists – readers
peers – peers!

All these groups apparently rely on the value and usefulness of communication, but among people who can be included in one of the two above columns: the left column, or the right column, and their interlocutors, huge asymmetries of information happen to exist, as well as inequalities on social and cultural levels, education, vocabulary proficiency...

Therefore, it is very important that the issuer of words, the leader, et cetera, communicate his/her **ideas**, projects, visions, recommendations, news, **orders**, in a language understandable by the individuals those ones are aimed at, and that he/she makes sure that what it has been said or recorded or printed can be clearly understood by the people receiving the message.

Though generally speaking the U.S. is a country with fairly high education indicators, American consumers buy junk food, junk entertainment, garbage stuff, and junk information... but in contrast, when it comes to junk politicians, citizens pay little attention to them, and consider there is not a meaningful alternative. Thus, many citizens "exercise" democracy every four years only.

In 1976, rock band Grand Funk Railroad released an album named *Born to Die*. It includes the song "Politician", written and composed by singer, guitarist and composer Mark Farner. A line of that song reads: "Mr. Politician please don't deceive us." That is just what every American could ask for when it comes to the political arena; after all, politicians make their best efforts to serve the nation, don't they?

From other perspective, the one of a politician, in 1973 the then-members of the Alice Cooper Band: Alice Cooper, Glen Buxton, Michael Bruce, Dennis Dunaway, and Neal Smith wrote, composed, arranged, performed and recorded the song "Elected" ("I wanna be elected…"). It was included in the album *Billion Dollar Babies*.

Everybody should know that politicians (supposedly) work mainly with their mind, vocal chords, mouth, pens or keyboards —mindwork and so-called light tasks, and not muscle power—, but it is the case that some of them wrongly exercise the powers that have been granted to them, just as authors, ghostwriters, scribes, copyists and journalists, sometimes do, although at a lower level, and therefore these ones cause less damage.

Besides, many U.S. citizens are brainwashed by the media, large corporations, the Internet; Hollywood films, which have been, are and will be produced, directed and starred mainly by Jews; soap operas, reality shows, beauty pageants, television shows, talk shows, sports,[3] the Government itself. All of us know that ignorance must be fought via accurate information, instruction, and education.

The discrepancy between what a human being **needs** and what he/she **wants** or even longs for, reflects the gap between reason and emotion.

---

3. Which indeed are not sports in the sense understood by ancient Olympic Greeks, whose only two awards for every winner were a laurel wreath on their temples and having their name engraved on a stone column (the fame). Please, compare this to the money an NFL or MLB player earns per year nowadays.

Picture this: you are at home or at the office. How would you feel if an acquaintance or a co-worker or a friend of you approached you and tried to draw your wallet and steal your bills?, how would you react?

Surely you would stop him/her and would invite him/her to leave your place and maybe would admonish him/her: "Never come back"…

Now, why do not you assess your TIME in a similar way? You let your time easily and thoughtlessly slip away when you are chatting, or wasting time on Facebook,® YouTube,® Instagram,® et cetera, or worse, watching television or playing electronic games. These are the main thieves of YOUR time. Don't you remember that "time is money"?

Most people **need** education in order to land well-paid jobs and contribute to a better society, but they **want** entertainment, pleasures, leisure, easy living, more money, et cetera.

The cohesive forces that maintain the Union are liberty, equality, Law, republicanism, democracy, federalism, unalienable individual rights, progress, tolerance, scientific and social progress, commitment to free markets, the U.S. Constitution, and a large body of constitutional law.

These elements constitute the fabric, the warp and woof of public life and relationships among the citizens of the United States of America.

Back in the 18th Century, several of the Founding Fathers of the U.S., dwelling in some of the Thirteen Colonies, until 1776 subject to the British Crown (George III, of the House of Hanover, was the King), mainly Thomas Jefferson and James Madison, the latter being considered as "the father of the U.S. Constitution", had read some of the books penned by English philosopher John Locke and also British poet and essayist John Milton, as well a treatise written by French Baron de La Brède et de Montesquieu.

The U.S. Constitution was written by James Madison, Thomas Jefferson, John Adams, Alexander Hamilton, Thomas Paine, and others, who lavishly took advantage of *Two Treatises of Government* (1690) a book penned by Locke[4] and, to a lesser extent, of *Areopagitica* (1644), an essay written by English parliamentarian turned Cromwellian and republican John Milton, as well as from a treatise on political theory, *The Spirit of the Laws* (*De L'Esprit des Loix*), published in 1748 by French historian and political thinker Charles-Louis de Secondat, Baron de La Brède et de Montesquieu, in which,

---

4. John Locke (1632-1704), the father of empiricism and modern liberalism, who influenced Montesquieu, proposed that "… sovereignty emanates from the people [not from God], that property, life, liberty and pursuit of happiness are men's natural rights, prior to the formation of society. The State has as main purpose to protect those rights, and also the individual freedoms of citizens." An Enlightenment thinker, Locke considered reason as the primary source of authority and legitimacy. It was no surprise that Locke's books were included in the *Index of Prohibited Books* (*Index Librorum Prohibitorum*) by the Holy Catholic Apostolic Roman Church.

influenced by Locke, he states that there must be a separation of powers.

The Legislative branch is responsible for making and enacting laws.

The Executive branch is responsible for implementing, enforcing, and administering the public policy enacted and funded by the Legislative branch.

The Judicial branch is responsible for interpreting the Constitution and laws and applying its interpretations to controversies brought before it.

It is not strange that during human interrelations, disputes and confrontations arise.

Two or more points of view compete against each other; several free citizens consider their rights are blocked or violated by others' rights.

Antithesis is the state of two things, judgments or claims that are directly opposite to each other

Some solutions can come out of confrontation, discussion, debate.

AN OLDE VOICE FROM THE DISTANT PAST

Ionic philosopher Heraclitus of Ephesus (c. 535-c.475 B.C. [BCE]) comes into play:

Είμαστε ταυτόχρονα βήμα και δεν βήμα στα ίδια ποτάμια.

"We both step and do not step in the same river."

A phrase that has been misrepresented as:

Δεν μπορούμε να το βήμα δύο φορές στο ίδιο ποτάμι.

"We cannot step twice in the same river."

One and Many: The Dialectics of Contraries in Heraclitus

Certainly the contraries are not a discovery of Heraclitus; prior to his philosophy, the Milesians[5] and, above all, the Pythagoreans, conceived opposites in their opposition and their individualized permanence facing each other; however, always from a static concept. It was Heraclitus who provided the radically new idea of the dialectic [dynamics] of contraries.

In the Heraclitean future, it is not about the transmutation of a particular exclusive reality into another also exclusive —though sometimes it has been interpreted that way—, but about the transition from one form to another —a transit which does not imply the annulment of opposites but their conflictual coexistence.

---

5. Heraclitus, however, did not accept the Milesian monism and replaced their underlying material arche with a single, divine law of the universe, which he called Logos (Λόγος) [Reason]. The universe of Heraclitus is in constant change, but also remaining the same.

The opposition and the union of contraries is what constitutes the perpetual motion; it is the troubled union of contraries which establishes the future, and it is not the future which moves them.

Heraclitus went on to stress one axiological, subjective contradiction according to which all values require [their respective] countervalues.

Being the same and the contrary successively is what constitutes the Heraclitean future.

The reciprocal implication of contraries, each of which is with its genesis and its death, a condition of death and genesis of the other, it can also be configured as its identity or unity.

3.
THE ECONOMY

A re both campaigns economy-centered?

Sort of.

The stressed nation is facing hard times, but despite their politicians, it will continue to be the #1 economy of the world, dusting China...[6] during a certain period.

---

6. A country inhabited by people which are counted among the ugliest human beings in the world, the Chinese... according to Western beauty canons, parameters and paradigms set, albeit involuntarily, by painters such as *il Pinturicchio* (Bernardino di Betto), Albrecht Dürer, Rembrandt, Diego Velázquez, John Waterhouse, et cetera. Besides, Chinese products and services are low-quality ones, and these happen to be reflections, fruits, out of their makers, low-end people.

No matter at all that a deep sinking of the world economy may be close to happen.

It is expected that China slow down more, and both the European Union (EU) and the United Kingdom weaken themselves, after the *successful* British exit (Brexit).

The Donald **Trump** tax plan includes:

Tax relief for middle class Americans.

Simplification of the tax code.

Grow the American economy by discouraging corporate inversions, adding a huge number of new jobs, and making America globally competitive again.

Doesn't add to our debt and deficit, which are already too large.

Trump's economic platform features three key elements: a large tax cut for all individuals and businesses, a tougher trade policy, and immigration reform. Make America Great Again!

While sometimes it could seem that Trump can't see the forest for the trees, the fact is that he only needs to walk backwards, to the top of the ridge, and watch the landscape.

However, in order to prevent an excess of immigrants from the brown wave, in the event that this grandson of four immigrant grandparents become President, he should consider choosing maybe one or two out of three options: (A) satellites, (B) thousands of drones implemented as instruments of surveillance in the South Border of the U.S., and (C) the building of an expensive wall.

For... some 38 percent of illegal Mexican and Hispanic immigration reaches the States by plane; then they overstay their visas and "camouflage" themselves among U.S. citizens and legal residents.

—

As some may know, instead of rejecting foreign products, opponents of globalization today are **rejecting foreign people**, but consumers should reject made abroad, foreign products as a sign of congruence —"Buy American"—. Oh, but low-priced products mean bargains. "Keep on saving, my friends, don't buy American!"

■

Hillary **Clinton** would opt for:

Give working families a raise, and tax relief that helps them manage rising costs.

Create good-paying jobs and get pay rising by investing in infrastructure, clean energy, and scientific and medical research to strengthen our economy and growth.

Close corporate tax loopholes and make the most fortunate pay their fair share.

This may be only an illusionary purpose.

—

"Tax the rich, feed the poor,/ 'til there are no rich no more"… these are two lines of the lyrics of "I'd Love to Change the World", a song composed and performed by British rock band Ten Years After.

This was only an illusion of the seventies.

Hillary Clinton had (or has?) plans to build… not a wall, but a fence:

http: // www [dot] investors [dot] com/politics/commentary/hillary-clinton-was-for-building-a-wall-with-mexico-before-she-was-against-it/

██████

But any of them could copy the Steve Forbes' 1996 proposal of a flat tax of 17 percent on all personal and corporate earned income, OR tax everyone with a scalable rate ranging from 9 to 45 percent, according to the amount of net income (please, see below: THE END OF TAX EVASION).

The House of Representatives would have to abolish some taxes: no fringe benefit tax, no stamp duty, no payroll tax, no sales tax...

██████

Also, the next President of the U.S. could authorize more government incentives to American wind farms, as well as to buyers and manufacturers of plug-in electric vehicles (PEVs), in order to beat conky Middle East crude oil producers.

∠ ∠ ∠

Above, "three Muslims" looking to the
left.

█████

THE END OF TAX EVASION

Also, the day when the dream of some
heads of the offices of the Internal
Revenue Service (IRS), and the
purposes of tax collectors in the U.S.
could come true might not be far from
now:

To put an end to fiscal elusion and
evasion by implementing a policy which
forbid the circulation of banknotes and
coins.

All of the money circulating in the U.S.
will have to be gradually removed and
forbidden, and every individual, every
inhabitant of the United States, including
infants, will receive a debit/credit card.
This will be a personal card which, when
inserted in an Automated Consult

Machine or Automated Teller Machine, will transfer certain data to an Automated Center of Transactions (ACT) located in, let's say, Pueblo, Colorado; Palo Alto, California; New York City, et cetera. The ACT will process and record all of the transactions authorized/made by any individual when using his/her Individual Card (IC).

Those Individual Cards (ICs), shall record absolutely all financial transactions:

accounts payable, accounts receivable, acquisitions, adjustments, alimony, allowances, amortizable intangible assets, amortization, assets, balances, barters, bills of exchange, bonds, bonuses, business inventory, capital increases, capital reductions, carrybacks, carryforwards, changes, collection costs/fees, collections, commissions, compensations, consolidations, constitution of companies, contracting, credit notes, credits, currency exchange, debits, debts, deductions, default interests, deferred tax assets, delivery notes, deposits, depreciation, differences, discounts, donations, down payments, dues, earnings, EBITDAs (Earnings Before Interest, Taxes, Depreciation, and Amortization), electronic funds transfers, equity, exchanges, expenses, fees, financial statements, financing, finder's fees, fines and penalties, funds, futures, gains, grants, income, inheritance, interests, interests earned, interests paid, investments, invoices, late fees, leasing, letters of credit, liabilities, liquidations, loans, losses, management fees, mergers, money orders, movements, net tangible assets, options on futures, overdue accounts, payment of dividends, payments, prepaid amounts, prizes, profits, professional fees, promissory notes, purchases, rebates, receipts, redemptions, refunds, registration balances, reimbursements, releases, remittances of money, returns, revenue, revolving funds, rights, royalties, salaries, sales, services, shipments, stipends, stock options, stocks, transactions, transfers, trusteeships, trusts, wages, withdrawals... et cetera.

Also, there will be credit/debit cards issued on behalf of corporations, banks, municipal governments, state governments, agencies, corporations, companies, associations, clubs, educational institutions, so that each company or entity will have a single card, and a single identification number.

So, the last day of each quarter (03/31, 06/30, 09/30, and 12/31) it could be automatically collected from citizens, residents, corporations and organizations around the country, a tax that could range from 9 to 45 percent, according to their net earnings. This tax might come to be known as the Quarterly Individual Tax (QIT) / Quarterly Corporation Tax (QCT) or a similar name.

(No more need to file tax returns, no need to buy expensive TurboTax® software or any other high-priced alternative.)

The software and metasoftware installed at the servers of the Automated Center of Transactions (ACT) shall be managing, storing and backing data and transactions, and creating and updating DATABASES, et cetera.

About data and information, such software will be able to fetch, parse, index, arrange, queue, retrieve, store, process, classify, manage, rank, query, build tables and graphics, build info trees, make multiple juxtapositions of data, search for intrinsic quality or "specific weight" of data, weigh relevance,[7] deliver and store reports, et cetera.

By issuing and implementing the use of Individual Cards (ICs), tax evasion shall be reduced to a minimum, and eventually will come to an end.

… And a new era of super-symbolic, intangible money will start.

Programmers, engineers, nerds and geeks could create the appropriate apps

---

7. Relevance could be construed on the basis of certain criteria as applied by utilizing pre-established financial and economic scales, tariffs and parameters.

to manage automated bookkeeping, accounting, and communication with the Automated Center of Transactions (ACT).

NO BROKERS

Besides, with the cooperation of the House of Representatives, the new President could help the investing public to get rid of financial brokers, and automate clearing and transactions at exchanges such as the Chicago Mercantile Exchange (CME), the New York Stock Exchange (NYSE), et cetera. So, investors, speculators, day traders, et cetera, could invest directly in stock exchanges, commodities exchanges, and financial markets, accelerate the pace of economy, and thus, make the markets grow.

RFID

Also, it should be considered that, be whoever the candidate who win, he/she would have to promote the development of better and more accurate radio-frequency identifiers (RFID), to increase its feasibility in order to make a more economic and wider use of them, and contribute to the betterment of production, commerce, and to help to reduce thefts.

XLIV

4.
DOMESTIC ISSUES

D

espite its rulers, the United States will continue thriving.

A recipe:

Citizens are very busy making money or earning a living, so they do not want or cannot implement self-management, or have no time; therefore, they badly need the intervention of politicians, who must take care of the people, and oversee that citizens do not become overburdened with absurd chores, red tape, et cetera.

Power is an irresistible magnet; many go after it, without minding to pay a very high price. They leave behind their health, peace of mind, even some of their personal relationships.

Democracies or dictatorships, nations have been led by small groups, oligarchies, elites, select minorities, who make important decisions not always seeking the benefit of the people.

—

The Nine Steps of Strategic Planning are as follows:

1. Diagnosis.
2. Objectives.
3. Goals.
4. Analysis of Resources and Obstacles.
5. Activities.
6. Personnel in Charge.
7. Time. Develop a Timetable, Gantt Charts, et cetera.
8. Implementation.
9. Evaluation.

There are many other recipes, "The Twelve Steps", "The Six Points", et cetera.

—

Some words about forward planning/strategic foresight:

Along with the probable implementation of quick solutions put into practice at the heat of the moment and perhaps for getting out well of conflicting occasions, I think it should be advisable for the forthcoming president, having handy, several hand-pickable, pre-designed, virtually pre-tested, algorithmically pre-evaluated, peer-reviewed, refereed, feed-backed, crossable, customizable, multi functional, omnidirectional, transectorial, multidisciplinary, multipurpose, substrates; maybe all of them virtual, epistemological ones.

—

From now until the final days of next October, the GOP should carefully consider organizing and running virtual and/or presential forums in order to get to know what the people's main concerns are.

An entrepreneur turned politician can approach politics and government duties from a citizens' perspective.

Sometimes, common people can become a politician's best advisors.

An Administration that can take solutions to the people will be qualified as successful.

A president, governor, mayor, et cetera, who is prepared to adopt the citizens' mindset will be fit and apt to solve or mitigate many people's problems.

One way to get citizens' feedback is by organizing and running open or select forums, no matter that the leaders of think tanks and war rooms of a given candidate decide to set the pace, themes, and even induce trends.

Ideas, analysis, thinking, discussion...

Forums can be moderated or not, and this is a decision that must be made by the candidate and his closest aides.

5.
THE GLOBAL ARENA

For the sake of Justice,
even the Law must be questioned.

The Worst Witch

T he "goodism" of the Right.

A HEGEMONIC NATION, AS USUAL —A CENTURY OF *PAX AMERICANA*

The globally dominant American Power
as everyone may know it today is a
maybe unexpected byproduct of
combined individual successes, self- and
mostly heterocircumstanced relativity,
the U.S. Constitution penned by James
Madison, Thomas Jefferson, et alii,
which provides the theoretical bases for
the Union and the cohesive legal force to

the Nation; assembly lines, mass production, machinery, capitalist ideology, accumulation of money, arms, knowledge, patents; investments, creation of opportunities, a free enterprise system, agriculture, cattle-raising, fisheries, mining, petroleum extraction and refining, foreign trade, et cetera, and last but not least, in the Course of World War I, an inexorable military power drift from the United Kingdom, its thalassocracy represented by the Admiralty, toward the United States.

The U.S. has exercised its world hegemony during a century.

But was the building of the U.S. a definite purpose, and if so, who were the first individuals to think about the great future of a Nation, and how far that New Republic would go?

Anyone can infer that in 1776, the attention of the Committee of Five: John Adams, representative of Massachusetts; Thomas Jefferson, representative of Virginia; Benjamin

Franklin, representative of Pennsylvania; Roger Sherman, representative of Connecticut; and Robert Livingston, representative of New York, had been centered less on the future of the new Nation than on the necessary breaking of political and economic ties with the British Crown, due to "injuries and usurpation", dissolutions of Representative Houses, "cutting off our Trade with all parts of the world", "imposing Taxes on us without our Consent", "He [the King] has plundered our seas, ravaged our coasts, burnt our towns, and destroyed the lives of our people."

The new country started to ride and thrive at high speed, in a non-subtle, fast evolution that unstoppably turned into a reason-science-and-technology-backed industrial, commercial, and sociopolitical revolution, taken into account, exploited and enjoyed by the new leader of the Anglosphere as of 1916, the most conspicuous of the British spin-offs —the United States; being the others: Canada, Australia, New Zealand—, which had come to control the steering wheel.

The Federal Reserve System (FRS),[8] the Atlantic Charter, the North Atlantic Treaty Organization (NATO); the General Agreement on Tariffs and Trade (GATT), its successor as of January 1, 1995: the World Trade Organization (WTO); the International Monetary Fund (IMF), the World Bank, et cetera, are institutions created or propelled by the U.S., and they serve as keepers of a paradoxically dynamic status quo ("If we want things to stay as they are, things will have to change." —*The Leopard* (Italian: *Il Gattopardo*), a novel by Italian author Giuseppe Tomasi di Lampedusa [1896-1957]).

By 1989, the communism and its pink-tinged half-sibling, the socialist system, started to collapse mostly from within, with some outside help from President Ronald Reagan, British Premier Margaret Thatcher, Pope John Paul II (Karol Wojtyla), and a wide array of allies.

8. Although some argue that the FRS is controlled by several European banks, these assertions have the appearance of being a fallacy, or are very difficult to prove.

Then, the U.S. drifted its somewhat tired eyes across the shore to see if it happened to discover any enemy worthy of respect, but... no, not a single one left.

The king of all nations felt itself more secure and started to drive freely in a brand new highway, perhaps evaded by the sweet smell of its reaffirmed leadership.

Now, when seen from the perspective of the abovementioned benchmarks — 1916, when the U.S. overtook the United Kingdom, and 1989, when the Union of Soviet Socialist Republics and the *Iron Curtain* were about to collapse— the forthcoming renovation of the higher spheres of the Executive branch seems a habitual task, an act in which a 538-headed magician wearing a black cloak handpicked out of his many wizard capes, by art of hocus pocus makes a new President appear out of a smoke and fog cloud... ready and desired, very apt to exercise power.
All of what the new President will have to do will just be to prove himself/herself

worthy of trust to preserve the economic, political and military hegemony of the United States, as well as its leadership in language —English is still the *lingua franca* of the planet—, mass media, technology, and culture,[9] despite his/her past misadventures, mistakes, and sometimes fluctuating weak-powerful drive.

Trump wants to build a wall a few feet North of the U.S. Southern border.

Clinton does not want a wall, but a fence.

---

9. In the fields of fashion, automotive design, industrial design, graphic design, right now the U.S. faces fierce competition from France, Italy, Spain, and England.

A CALAMITY: MUSLIMS

—Is there something worse than
a fly in an operating room?
—Yes, two flies in an operating room.

It is well-known that some centuries ago the Muslim world shone, and even eclipsed some other cultures. Muslims created **Algebra**, took the zero (0), invented in India, to Europe through Italy, made big contributions to Chemistry via scientific research and Alchemy, as well as to Astronomy. It was the Arabs who perfected the recipe for soap by combining vegetable oils with sodium hydroxide (NaOH). Islamic architects invented the pointed arch (which gave origin to the Gothic arch in

Europe) and the ribbed vaulting… but after some centuries, the Islamic Civilization declined and was surpassed by the Western Civilization.

The clearing of the "x" by following the method of completing the perfect square is shown below:

$$ax^2 + bx + c = 0$$

$$(ax^2 + bx + c)\,4a = (0)\,4a$$

$$4a^2x^2 + 4abx + 4ac = 0$$

$$4a^2x^2 + 4abx + 4ac - 4ac = 0 - 4ac$$

$$4a^2x^2 + 4abx = -4ac$$

$$4a^2x^2 + 4abx + b^2 = -4ac + b^2$$

$$4a^2x^2 + 4abx + b^2 = b^2 - 4ac$$

$$(2ax + b)^2 = b^2 - 4ac$$

$$2ax + b = \pm\sqrt{b^2 - 4ac}$$

$$2ax + b - b = \pm\sqrt{b^2 - 4ac}\ - b$$

$$2ax = \pm\sqrt{b^2 - 4ac}\ - b$$

$$2ax = -b \pm\sqrt{b^2 - 4ac}$$

$$\frac{2ax}{2a} = \frac{-b \pm \sqrt{b^2 - 4ac}}{2a}$$

$$x = \frac{-b \pm \sqrt{b^2 - 4ac}}{2a}$$

The above is known as the general algebraic formula for quadratic equations or second-degree equations.

—

Islam ("submission"), as their religion is called, is as false and poorly structured as a cardboard coin. It is an erroneous and dangerous religion. And the worst is that they [the Muslims] exercise a continuous, violent, and fanatically induced proselytism.

Since the death of the founder of their faith, they split into two main divisions: (A) Sunnis, 84 percent of the worldwide Muslim population) —their religious allegiance and discipleship is toward

Allah and Muhammad, but through the interpretations of the latter's father-in-law, Abu Bakr—; Sunni successor is called a Caliph, and (B) Shiites, 14 percent —their religious allegiance and discipleship is also toward Allah and Muhammad, but through the interpretations of Muhammad's son-in-law and first cousin Ali ibn Abi Talib—; Shiite successor is called an Imam. Each faction fights the contrary, the "fraternal" enemy, and they have started several intra-religious wars.

Radical Muslims are highly fanatic people, violent ones, frequently burst in flares of rage, and a lethal danger for the world.

All male Muslims are considered, from a Western viewpoint, as repressors of women's rights.

Many Muslims simply cannot avoid showing their big noses and ugly nostrils.

The Islamic lunar calendar is a crap!

Following, some wars, battles, skirmishes, and bomb explosions, which have been part of *clashes of civilizations*[10] are mentioned:

711–788. Muslims invaded and conquered the Visigothic Kingdom in the Iberian Peninsula (Spain and Portugal).

732. They were defeated by French ruler Charles Martell near Poitiers, France. Martell saved most of Western European Civilization from Muslim conquest.

11th to 15th centuries. Muslims defeated the invading Crusaders (Christian forces) in Palestine and the rest of the Middle East.

1492. Muslims were defeated and expelled from Spain by the armed forces of the Queen of Castile and León, Isabella I of the House of Trastámara, and her husband, the King of Aragón,

---

10. A conceptual phrase coined by Western scholar Bernard Lewis. From an Aussie source: http: // mailstar [dot] net/huntington [dot] html

Ferdinand II of the Aragonese Branch of the House of Trastámara.

October 7, 1571. The Ottoman Empire was defeated by the Holy League (a Christian coalition formed by the Republic of Venice, the Papal States, the Spanish Empire, the Kingdom of Naples, the Kingdom of Sicilia, the Great Duchy of Tuscany, and others forces), led by admiral Don Juan of Austria, in the maritime Battle of Lepanto (Greece), though the fleet of Sultan Selim II quickly recovered itself in six months, and from 1573 the Ottomans again controlled the Mediterranean. In August 1574, they regained the territory of Tunisia, who had been under the control of the Spanish Empire of King Felipe II, of the House of Habsburg.

November 30, 1853. During the Crimean War, Tsar Nicholas I Romanov sent warships which destroyed the Ottoman (Turkish) fleet at the Battle of Sinope, in the homonymous port, located on the north coast of Turkey, in the Black Sea.

November 5, 1854. France and Great Britain formed a short-lived alliance with the Ottoman Empire, because they wanted to prevent the fall of the latter, and so tackle the excessive Russian expansionism. The Allies defeated the Russians in the land battle of Inkerman, near Sevastopol, in the Crimean Peninsula.

1916-1918. British captain Lawrence of Arabia helped in the organization of the Arab Revolt against the Ottoman Empire. Fourteen years after (1932), the Kingdom of Saudi Arabia was created.

May 1948. Egypt, Jordan, Syria, Lebanon, Saudi Arabia and Iraq were defeated by Israel Army and Air Force.

June 5-10, 1967. Egypt was defeated by Israel in the Six Days War.

October 6, 1973. Egypt and Syria were defeated by Israel in the Yom Kippur War.

March 11, 1978. Palestinian militants landed on beach near Haifa, Israel; shot civilians and hijacked bus with hostages to Tel Aviv; 43 killed.

November 20, 1979. Islamic radicals seized Grand Mosque in Mecca, Saudi Arabia, and held hundreds of pilgrims hostage; Saudi forces retook mosque December 4; about 240 died.

April 18, 1983. Hezbollah suicide truck bomb exploded at the U.S. Embassy in Beirut, Lebanon; 63 died.

October 23, 1983. Hezbollah suicide truck bombings of U.S. and French military bases, Beirut; 242 Americans and 58 French killed.

December 21, 1988. Pan Am Flight 103 exploded over Lockerbie, Scotland; all 259 aboard and 11 on the ground died. Libya accepted responsibility for bombing in August, 2003.

February 26, 1993. Truck bomb activated by Al-Qaeda members exploded in World Trade Center garage in New York City; 6 killed.

September 11, 2001. Nineteen Al-Qaeda terrorists hijacked four U.S. domestic flights, including two planes that crashed into World Trade Center towers in New York City and one into Pentagon; death toll: 2,973 plus 19 terrorists.

March 11, 2004. Al-Qaeda terrorists bombed four commuters trains in Madrid, Spain; 191 killed.

July 7, 2005. Four bombs exploded on three separate subways and a bus in London; 52 killed.

April 15, 2013. Boston Marathon. 3 killed, some 262 injured.

January 7, 2015. *Charlie Hebdo Magazine* headquarters, Paris, attacked. 12 killed.

November 13, 2015. Paris. Six coordinated terrorist attacks. 130 killed.

December 2, 2015. San Bernardino, California. A Muslim couple killed 14, injured 22.

December 31, 2015–January 1, 2016. Germany. During the New Year's Eve celebrations, hundreds of sexual assaults (including groping), numerous thefts, and at least five rapes were reported, mainly in Cologne city centre. Similar incidents were reported in Hamburg, Frankfurt, Dortmund, Düsseldorf, Stuttgart, and Bielefeld. Police reported that the perpetrators were men of "Arab or North African appearance".

March 22, 2016. Brussels, Belgium. Three coordinated bombings occurred. 32 killed, over 300 injured. Islamic State of Iraq and the Levant (ISIL) claimed responsibility for the attacks.

June 12, 2016. Orlando, Florida. 49 killed, 53 injured in a gay nightclub shooting perpetrated by a Muslim American of Afghan descent.

July 14, 2016. Nice, France. A Tunisian resident of France deliberately drove a 19-tonne cargo truck into crowds celebrating the 227th Anniversary of Bastille Day (Tuesday, July 14, 1789) on the Promenade des Anglais, in Nice, killing 85 people and injuring 202.

And so on.

The Islamic "golden age" came to an end in the 15th century, and while the Muslim world sank in its own "Dark Ages" —which started in the 16th century and continue until today—, European powers used to fight each other (the Papal States included), and these beneficial tension, give-and-take, and swinging forces were of paramount importance in the rising of Western Civilization, facilitated European preponderance over Islam, and eventually strengthened the supremacy of the West in world culture, reinforced by the 18th century Industrial Revolution.

Stubborn and illiterate Muslims cannot abide the fact that Western values of democracy, free markets, separation of church and State,[11] individualism, limited

---

11. Accordingly, when it comes to separation of State and Church, it would be better to follow an obvious command (for some, suggestion) coming from Jesus-Christ: "Give to Caesar what is

government, and the rule of law, are long-standing <u>institutions</u> which shall not be brought down of the road.

What Muslims see as a detriment, Westerners view as an improvement for the world, and vice versa.

A dialogue can not be held between deaf people. Wars will continue until the end of the world.

It is a well-known fact that Domestic Perversity Index (DPI) is higher in Muslim countries than in Western nations.

Caesar's, and to God what is God's." *Matthew*, 22, 21. —"Reddite ergo, quae sunt Caesaris, Caesari et, quae sunt Dei, Deo." Evangelium secundum Matthaeum, XXII, 21, and the ideas concerning that point, Dutch philosopher Baruch Spinoza (1632-1677) exposed in Chapter VI of his *Political Treatise*, in which he unequivocally establishes the separation of Church and State: "As far as religion concerns, no church shall be built at the expense of cities, and no law shall be enacted respecting a religious belief, unless it is seditious and undermine the foundations of the State. The faithful authorized to publicly practice their worship, if they want churches, they will build them at their expense."

The Domestic Perversity Index (DPI) of a given country can be calculated by multiplying the **annual** number of murders per 1,000 population, by the number of sentenced delinquents per 1,000 population, by the number of all kinds of felonies, frauds, crimes, et cetera (excluding homicides), per 1,000 population, by the percentage of the economically active population that works in informality, id est, does not pay taxes, by the cost of corruption expressed as a percentage of the Gross Domestic Product (GDP), by the Gini Coefficient.

In most Muslim countries, a secular State simply does not exist, there is neither freedom of worship nor to express atheism and women are oppressed and treated as minors and even slaves. Polygyny is legal. The thousands of fool dhimwits[12] living in

---

12. Dhimwit: A non-Muslim member of a free society that abets the stated cause of Islamic domination with remarkable gullibility or guile. A dhimwit is always quick to extend sympathy to the very enemy that would take away his/her own freedom (or life) if given the opportunity.

Western countries ought to be aware of these facts.

ANOTHER CALAMITY: JEWS

Judaism is another false religion, like a lead coin.

After the destruction of most of the city of Jerusalem by one of the Roman armies in 70 C.E., the Jewish diaspora ("Roman exile" or "Edom exile") started.

Since then, wherever they have gone and settled, Jews have tried —and in many cases have achieved— to control and dominate politics, government, economy, financing, banking, moneylending!, mining, steel production, building activities, oil refining, entertainment (show business), agriculture, food processing, many other industries, commerce, mass media, internet, et cetera, et cetera.

Some enemies of the Jews have been:
Babylonians, Assyrians, Chaldeans,
Amalekites, Philistines, Jebusites,
Egyptians, Greeks, Romans (the Roman
Gold Eagle subdued them for centuries),
Spaniards (the Jews were expelled from
Spain by the Catholic Monarchs
Ferdinand of Aragon and Isabella of
Castile in 1492), Russians (numerous
pogroms), Nazi Party members
(**Na**tionalso**zi**alistische Deutsche
Arbeiterpartei; National Socialist German
Workers Party) during the Third Reich,
1933-1945; Syrians, Iranians, Arabs,
Muslims...

Unconditional or almost unconditional
hatred toward Jews has been
widespread, but not for free: it has had a
high price.

Abhorrence and contempt also abound,
and, on the other hand, commiseration
and compassion, when they have
suffered massacres, banishments,
segregation, isolation, racial laws,
refusal to enter a country,
socioeconomic barriers, disparagement,
abound toward these people (Hebrews,

Israelites, Jews) whose origins lie in certain desert areas of Asia, some territories of the Middle East.

Many descendants of patriarch Jacob, after more than 3,700 years, do not consider victorious themselves; it seems that sometimes they are invaded by uneasiness, huge concern, uncertainty, and confusion.

Oh, Henry Ford (1863-1947)!

Oh, *The Dearborn Independent* (1925)!

Those of them who are millionaires live with the comfort and luxuries that their high socioeconomic status allows them to do so.

A racial stereotype: Jews have "Jewish six" noses, big noses, "Jewish nostrils"… and therefore, many? Jewish girls of means enter operating rooms of plastic surgeons to get rhinoplasty done, and so they can brag about having gotten a brand-new Greek nose or straight nose.

Nose reshaping at its best.

∠ ∠

Above, a "stylized drawing" of the respective noses (l - r) of two Jews who "were looking" to the left: Mayer Amschel Bauer (who changed his family name to Rothschild, "Red Shield", 1744-1812) and Bernard Baruch (1870-1965).

Mediterranean (Greek, Italian, French, et cetera) and other goyisheh women with big noses —or "Jewish noses"— want also to look like pretty WASPs, so they have requested rhinoplasty too.

Do you know the differences between Anti-Islamism, Anti-Semitism (an ambiguous word which should be avoided), Anti-Judaism, and Anti-Zionism? If not, you should.

—

Stratfor —an Austin-based "global intelligence company"— sells info which otherwise can be googled or gathered from free sources, at very high prices. It was founded and once chaired by Jewish-Hungarian researcher and geopolitical forecaster George Friedman (Budapest, 1949-).[13]

—

The Irgun, a Zionist paramilitary and terrorist organization, operated in Mandate Palestine between 1931 and 1948.

July 22, 1946. Bombing of the King David Hotel in Jerusalem. 91 killed, 46 injured.

April 9, 1948. The Deir Yassin massacre, carried out by the Irgun together with the Lehi (also a Zionist organization). 107 killed. Deir Yassin was a Palestinian Arab village.

---

13. Stratfor is a joke. http: // www [dot] theatlantic [dot] com/international/archive/2012/02/stratfor-is-a-joke-and-so-is-wikileaks-for-taking-it-seriously/253681/

A young Menachem Begin (1913-1992), once a member of the Irgun, was a terrorist too. He served as Prime Minister of Israel from 1977 to 1983.

■

Some events of Christian terrorism.

1605. The Gunpowder Plot (London).

1648. Khmelnytsky Uprising or Cossack-Polish War, in Ukraine and Belarus. Some 144,000 Orthodox Christian, Jews, and Catholics killed.

1865–1870s, 1915–1944, and 1946–2014. Ku Klux Klan (United States). 3,446 blacks killed.

1821, 1859, 1871, 1881, 1886, 1905. Several pogroms in Czarist Russia. State terrorism. The wide span of numbers goes from several hundreds to approximately 60,000 Jews killed.

1930. Pogroms in Romania.

1971-2008. Irish Republican Army (IRA) attacks death toll: about 1,800 killed.

—

Atheism is better, atheists say; Hinduism is better, Hindus announce; Judaism is better, Jews think; Christianity is better, Christians state; Islam is better, Muslims proclaim, et cetera.

The highest degree of proselytism is watched in Islam, the second highest one belongs to Christianity.

ORDO AB CHAOS

*"Nothing in this world can take
the place of persistence.*

*"Talent will not: nothing is more common than
unsuccessful men with talent.*

*"Genius will not: unrewarded
genius is almost a proverb.*

*"Education will not: the world is
full of educated derelicts.*

*"Persistence and determination
alone are omnipotent."*

—Calvin Coolidge (1872-1933)

The world would be very boring and
rather more predictable if everything
were in order and worked close to
perfection *per se*, "inherently". That way,
the work and the tasks started and
performed by mankind would be useless
and without a purpose; such activities
would have no reason to exist, other
than the glitter for the performers.

Therefore, juxtaposition or combination or <u>coexistence</u> of chaos (or disorder or entropy) and order is better for mankind and the Earth in general.

Life is "as is"... and that way, human work, efforts, struggle, fight, and progress have become more useful, significant, logic and even necessary.

Now, abuses and human-created entropy (chaos), when they cause damages to the environment, the biosphere, other human beings, are equal to evil, even if that little and/or confined chaos is not intended to do harm, and either it has come out of negligence, ignorance, haste, misconceptions, misunderstandings, or malice, egoism, et cetera: the result comes out the same: it causes damage to others.

The fight for survival is connatural to all living beings; what is alive, fights; interactions are unavoidable.

While chaos and order do coexist —not that they are intususceptioned, but only juxtaposed as a coalesced couple— the "goodism" of the Right tends to attack/dissipate chaos by turning and re-arranging its elements, and so a partial order is created out of a majority of chaos. History has proven that the Left has always shown tendencies to create more chaos and turbulence, although camouflaged as "progress".

Ordo ab chaos, albeit there is more chaos than order in the universe, so we can assume that there are many pending duties, jobs, tasks, to be completed during the years and centuries ahead.

Entities like the Association of Lions Clubs, International; Service To Mankind (Sertoma), Rotary International, et cetera, go on to help the overlooked, the needy, the less fortunate ones.

One of the foremost reasons of the existence of mankind is the transformation of reality by seeing, perceiving, thinking, planning, acting, working.

If mankind's tasks and endeavors have to be performed within a framework of Ethics, this is more imperative when it comes to the work of politicians.

EVIL TURNS AGAINST ITSELF

French sociologist and philosopher Jean Baudrillard (1929-2007) has asserted that the Western Civilization, "individuals, society and indeed the global system, are internally and irreconcilably divided, that modernity is 'at odds with itself'. In his view dissent, rejection and insurrection emerge from within, not from external challenges such as alternative ideologies or competing worldviews, but from within bodies, within borders, inside programmes. For Baudrillard, much of the violence, hatred and discomfort visible around the globe can be understood as a latent but fundamental 'silent insurrection' against the global integrating system and its many pressures, demands and humiliations. This is an endogenic or intra-genic rejection, it emanates from within the system, from within individuals..."

—Doctor William Pawlett, Media and Cultural Studies, University of Wolverhampton, United Kingdom.)

http: // www2 [dot] ubishops [dot] ca/baudrillardstudies/vol-11_2/v11-2-pawlett.html

They do not see that good never comes from a purification of evil (evil always retaliates in a forceful way), but rather from a subtle treatment which turns evil against itself.[14]

—Jean Baudrillard

Ils n'ont pas compris que le bien ne résulte jamais d'une éviction du mal, qui prend toujours alors une revanche

14. This phrase originally appeared in "La conjuration des imbéciles", in the French daily newspaper *Libération*, May 7, 1997.

http: // www [dot] liberation [dot] fr/tribune/1997/05/07/opposer-a-le-pen-la-vituperation-morale-c-est-lui-laisser-le-privilege-de-l-insolence-la-conjuration_206413 éclatante, mais d'un traitement subtil du mal par le mal.

■

TRUMP IS THE LEAST BAD

Voters should cast their respective ballots for Donald Trump after having read what Andrew C. McCarthy[15] has unmistakably written about "an ingenious way [the U.S. has] of nudging wayward personalities to do the right things."

Oh, William F. Buckley (1925-2008)!

You can look for the hashtag #TrumpRevolution in Twitter

---

15. Andrew C. McCarthy is a senior policy fellow at the National Review Institute and a contributing editor of National Review.
http: / /www [dot] nationalreview [dot] com/article/436206/conservatives-2016-donald-trump-hillary-clinton-david-french-obama

6.
THE PRESS, THE FOURTH ESTATE

Journalists, editors, publishers who work at several big daily newspapers are skilled and powerful enough as to raise clamors when it comes to prevent someone from reaching a position, so expect they will surely do their best toward Donald Trump not becoming the 45th President of the U.S.

Now, does the U.S. need a transition from an ethico-fugal society to an ethico-petal society?

Not exactly, as it is not the case that America be an ethico-fugal society, but rather a chiaroscuro, light and shade highly contrasted in certain areas, while other zones show some kind of gray-colored entities, an intertwined mixture of black and white.

7.
A JAPANESE IMAGINARY GAME

P lease, imagine a symbolic electronic game in which:

There are twenty avatars with distinctive colors, dressed in colorful costumes of karate, which have different and specific powers, and each one represents something, a characteristic part of each nominee:

1. His/her ego.
2. His/her imagination, ideas.
3. The awareness of his/her existence.
4. His/her will, the backbone of his/her spirit.
5. His/her spirit of service.
6. The attribute of understanding.
7. Reflection.
8. Speculation (futurism).
9. A mirage.

10. His/her hologram, which represents self-discipline —it is a two-dimensional (2D) hologram, we have to add. No 3D here.

11. His/her mind.

12. His/her soul —invisible, off, or very distant.

13. His/her fountain pen or sharpened pencil.

14. His/her vision.

15. His/her mirror —his/her knowledge of himself/herself and of the world.

16. His/her sword —his/her power, qualities, and strength.

17. A jewel of fine green jade (his/her riches).

18. His/her memory.

19. His/her creativity.

20. His/her brain —as a material receptacle of neurons, dendrites, somas, axons, synapses, molecules, atoms, it is the hardware for the avatar/element number 11, which is the software.

Elements 15, 16, and 17, represent valuable imperial regalia (knowledge, power, and riches) created by the goddess Amaterasu —Japanese divinity of the Sun and the universe; her name means "shining in the sky", who bequeathed the three objects to her grandson Ninigi, who in turn was great-grandfather of the mythical founder and first emperor of Japan, Jimmu (02/13/711-04/09/585 B.C. [BCE]), who supposedly lived 126 years and reigned during 75 years, from 03/11/660 to 04/09/585 B.C. (BCE), that is, until the day of his death.

Pursuant to the nowadays situation, delegates might consider worth trying to "play" the game in their mind, and then, cast their ballot after having chosen who they consider the best candidate to lead and serve the Nation.

LXXXVI

8.
TWO CONSIDERATIONS FOR FUTURE ELECTIONS

Electoral equity as per age of voters.

In this scheme of counting the value of the votes differentiated and proportional to citizens' age at the time of an election, the votes of individual voters (registered citizens) would have different values according to their age: for example, the vote of a voter who is 18 years old would be worth 0.18 votes, the vote of a voter 50 years old would be worth 0.50 votes, the vote of an elector 100 years old would be worth 1 vote, the vote of an elector 118 years old would be worth 1.18 votes, and so on... "Because adults have lived more and have experience."

For this calculation, the above rule would be applied according to the age of full years that a individual voter have on election day (primaries), without considering fractions of years.

On the other hand, an opposite approach to the above-described one could be applied instead, and thus the vote of an elector who is 18 years old would be worth exactly 1 vote, the vote of a voter 19 years old would be worth 0.99 votes, the vote of an individual who is 20 years old would be worth 0.98 votes, the vote of an elector 27 years old would be worth 0.91 votes, the vote of a voter 42 years old would be worth 0.76 votes, the vote of an elector 65 years old would be worth 0.53 votes, the vote of a voter 95 years old would be worth 0.23 votes, the vote of an elector 100 years old would be worth 0.18 votes, et cetera... "Because the young have almost all their promissory future 'unused', so many years to live."

9.
REPUBLICAN NATIONAL CONVENTION, DEMOCRATIC NATIONAL CONVENTION

Power tends to corrupt, and absolute power corrupts absolutely.

Lord Acton (1834-1902)

Trump has emerged strengthened after his nomination and his unusually long acceptance speech (75 minutes), on Thursday, 07/21/2016.

Meanwhile, Clinton has come weakened out of the Democratic National Convention because a cheater Debbie Wasserman Schultz stepped down as chairman of the Democratic National Committee after the party's convention, held July 25–28, 2016, at the Wells Fargo Center in Philadelphia.

One of the main features of the Democratic National Convention was an announced and expected stellar speak lineup, with some prestigious politicians/orators who backed candidate Clinton.

But... Realpolitik has got some bad news for her campaign, the Democratic Party militants, supporters, lackey, and sycophant press, especially Jew-owned daily newspapers based in the Big Apple, the Murder Capital of America, and the Windy City:

The mere very fact that the democratic candidate had received such kind of verbal support during the freak parade in Philadelphia was symptomatic of her weakness.

Wasserman has acknowledged her involvement to promote an intra-party rise of former Secretary of State Hillary Clinton over the pre-candidacy of democratic socialist Senator Sanders (Brooklyn, New York City, 09/08/1941-).

With that kind of cheaters as [former] collaborators, Clinton has turned into a suspect of applying a loose control over certain matters, mismanagement, or worse, complicity in the filthy maneuvers to achieve the defenestration of former pre-candidate Sanders.

The "size" of her fears about not becoming the "chosen one" among democrats was determining and directly proportional towards the "size" of cheating played against a formidable and overwhelming adversary Senator Bernie Sanders.

If this power-hungry woman, the rightful owner of a sometimes trembling and hesitating voice, more appropriate for and justifiable in an octogenarian lady, becomes the 45th President of the U.S., maybe that country will not be taken to a catastrophe, but the economy will go worse, and "**budgetivore**" politicians will feel free to run at high speed to their particular kingdom of neglect, breach, mess and failure, while enjoying the good life they like.

The current Administration is transparent as mud; should Hillary Clinton win the 58th quadrennial U.S. presidential election to be held on Tuesday, November 8, 2016, the nation will be immersed in a mud sea as of Friday, January 20, 2017.

10.
2016 PRESIDENTIAL DEBATES

G iven that *ars politica* can be considered a combination of the exercise of power by politicians and the perception by the public, the forthcoming 2016 presidential debates between Hillary Clinton and Donald Trump will be crucial and to a great extent determining of the U.S. presidential election's outcome, next Fall.

While the debates will not involve any actual exercise of power, they will allow for some glimpses about the whats and hows of such [future] exercise.

As both candidates belong to the Establishment, and generally speaking do not look for shaking the status quo, a verbal give-and-take between two elitists is expected.

It remains to be seen if during the debates, Donald Trump manages to attract more voters among yuppies, immigrants and millennials, as among rednecks and Southern conservatives he will apparently get a majority of voters.

In the first and third debates, topics will be selected by the respective to-be-announced moderators, while during the second debate, half of the questions will be posed directly by citizen participants and the other half will be posed by a to-be-announced moderator based on topics of broad public interest as reflected in social media and other sources.

The debates will air from 9:00 pm to 10:30 pm ET, and will be watched by millions.

First presidential debate.
Monday, September 26, 2016.
Venue: Hofstra University; Hempstead, New York.

Second presidential debate.
Sunday, October 9, 2016.
Venue: Washington University in St.
Louis; Saint Louis, Missouri.

Third presidential debate.
Wednesday, October 19, 2016.
Venue: University of Nevada, Las
Vegas; Las Vegas, Nevada.

XCVI

11.
THREE ACROSTICS

Confused she stood amidst the fog
Liars, there were many in town
Indeed good teachers were they
Nobody knew about her dark maneuvers
To rampantly and stubbornly excel
Over all the adversaries she might face
Niceties would be fine to know, but she refused.

Triumphant in business has he come
Reckless investments has he profited from
Union 'round him is what he looks for
Many raised hands should be put to work
Prompting the nation to a higher stand.

Socialist he says his ideology is
Anglo-Saxon his bloodline is not
Never would he deny his Jewish descent
Deeds needed, for well-being and equality
End of corporate abuses he seeks
Roaring money lions have disliked him
So maybe he should have tried harder.

Sanders used to fill his agenda with high ideals, while Hillary Clinton fills her head with germs of new lies, and Trump fills his vaults with money.

In the U.S., more than in other countries, money has turned into an important measuring gauge of success.

Alejandro Ochoa G.
August, 2016.
Gvadalaxara.

alheoc [at] hotmail [dot] com

Author is a Web 2.0 dilettante, *wordcaster*, info broker, former Spanish-language proofreader, Mexican archive clerk, bureaucrat.

Please, excuse me for any Grammar errors, and typos. Shakespeare's language is not my mother tongue.